The OlympKNITS

Laura Long

D&C
David and Charles

Contents

Introduction — 4

Reg the Runner — 6

Wayne the Weightlifter — 14

Gloria the Gymnast — 22

Bill and Bob the Boxers — 30

Cindy the Cyclist — 38

Fiona the Fencer — 46

Edward the Equestrian — 54

with Harry the Handsome Horse — 60

Kato the Karateka — 68

Rod, Rich, Rick and Ron the Rowers — 76

Su, Sal, Sim, Sam and Sven the Swimmers — 84

Suppliers — 94

About the Author — 94

Acknowledgments — 95

Index — 95

Introduction

Sport and knitting are my 2 passions. Without one or the other I would feel lost. So having the opportunity to write a book combining both is a match made in heaven! By knitting dolls in different coloured yarns, changing their hair and making their easy-to-sew sports outfits, you can create whole teams of competitors ready to take on one of the greatest sporting events in the world.

Sewing the outfits for each of your dolls enables you to create extra detail that is hard to achieve with knitting alone. Even if you are an amazing knitter and can make every detail, there is still something rather lovely about the combination of knitting and

sewing being used together to make a wonderful finished project. I use this practice in all the dolls I sell, too. When designing the dolls' outfits I researched each sport and tried to re-create the way the competitors dressed in miniature. The result is that the outfits you will create really convey the 'look' of the sports the knitted athletes are representing.

All the clothes have been developed in the simplest way so they are fun and quick to make, and many of the outfits can be made using oddments of fabric or old clothes. Worn-out swimming costumes are perfect for recreating the swimmer and cyclist outfits, and an

old white t-shirt is ideal for the rowers and weightlifter. Be inventive with the fabrics you choose – the brighter the raw materials, the more interesting the clothes will be.

The outfits are designed to fit a doll approximately 33cm (13in) tall. If your dolls are taller or shorter, all you need to do is make some basic alterations to the clothes. If your dolls are smaller, simply take in more of the seams when sewing the clothes together. If they are larger, leave a bit of a gap when cutting around the pattern.

Several months ago I put out a plea on my 'Laura Long Knitting' Facebook and Twitter pages calling for help with knitting the dolls for this book. I was absolutely amazed at the response.

I had people contact me from all over the country, and indeed the world, wanting to help. Despite having been created using the same pattern on the same sized needles, each doll was unique. It is this randomness that I love about knitting. The imperfections provide the personality and characters of the dolls. So don't panic if your dolls don't quite resemble those in the photographs here – that's the beauty of hand knitting!

Reg the Runner

Needles

4mm (US size 6) knitting needles

Yarn

50g (2oz) oatmeal DK (this will make 2 dolls)
Oddments of brown yarn for hair, brown or black for eyes and pink for mouth

Other materials

Stuffing
White t-shirt fabric for vest (an old t-shirt works very well for this)
Contrasting coloured thread for vest
Paper for number badge
Navy silk or satin for shorts
Contrasting coloured thread for shorts

White felt for shoes
Contrasting coloured thread for shoes
Ribbon and white yarn for shoes

Gauge

22sts and 30 rows to 10cm (4in)

NOTE ON GAUGE
All knitters have slightly different gauge, so it's important to check your gauge so that the outfit your athlete will wear fits properly. If you have more than the stated sts/rows to your 10cm (4in) swatch, then use slightly larger needles. If fewer, use slightly smaller needles.

Finished size

Approximately 33cm (13in) tall.

Abbreviations

K2tog knit the next 2 stitches together
Kfb knit forward and back into the same stitch to make 2 stitches
P2tog purl the next 2 stitches together
Rep repeat
Skpo slip 1, knit 1, pass the slipped stitch over the knitted stitch

Pattern

Head, body and legs

Start at top of head.
Cast on 7 sts.
Row 1 [Kfb] 6 times, k1 (13 sts).
Row 2 P.
Row 3 [Kfb, k1, kfb] 4 times, k1 (21 sts).
Row 4 P.
Row 5 [Kfb, k3, kfb] 4 times, k1 (29 sts).
Row 6 P.
Row 7 K6, [kfb] 2 times, k12, [kfb] 2 times, k7 (33 sts).
Row 8 P.
Rows 9–22 Stocking/stockinette stitch.
Row 23 K6, skpo, k2tog, k12, skpo, k2tog, k7 (29 sts).
Row 24 P.
Row 25 [K2tog, k3, skpo] 4 times, k1 (21 sts).
Row 26 P.

Row 27 K.
Row 28 P.
Body
Row 29 [Kfb, k1] rep to last st, [kfb] (32 sts).
Row 30 P.
Rows 31–54 Stocking/stockinette stitch.
Row 55 [K2tog, k1] rep to last 2 sts, k2tog (21 sts).
Row 56 P.
Legs
Row 57 K9, k2tog, turn (hold left leg sts and continue on 10 sts for right leg).
Row 58 P.
Rows 59–88 Stocking/stockinette stitch.
Feet
Row 89 K4, [kfb] 2 times, k4 (12 sts).
Row 90 P.
Row 91 K5, [kfb] 2 times, k5 (14 sts).
Row 92 P.
Row 93 K6, [kfb] 2 times, k6 (16 sts).
Row 94 P2tog, p12, p2tog (14 sts).
Row 95 K2tog, k10, k2tog (12 sts).
Row 96 [P2tog] rep to end of row (6 sts).
Thread yarn through remaining sts. Rep on remaining 10 sts for left leg.

Arms (make 2)

Cast on 10 sts.

Rows 1–30 Stocking/stockinette stitch.

Hands

Row 31 K1, [kfb] 2 times, k3, [kfb] 2 times, k2 (14 sts).

Row 32 P.

Rows 33–36 Stocking/stockinette stitch.

Row 37 [K2tog] rep to end of row (7 sts).

Thread yarn through remaining sts.

Making up

Head, body and legs

The head, body and legs are knitted all in one.

Sew down the back of the body and head and fill with stuffing.

Sew down the inner legs to the tips of the toes. Fill with stuffing as you go as the legs are thin.

Arms

Sew up the arm seams, filling with stuffing as you go.

Sew the arms on to the body using the neck shaping to help with positioning.

Hair

Thread a long length of yarn onto a thick needle (I used 2 lengths of yarn to make it quicker).

Sew 1cm (½in) stitches around the edge of the head to form the shape of the hairline. Try to work the stitches in the direction that real hair takes.

Fill in the gaps with more stitches until the whole head is covered.

Facial features

Embroider eyes using brown or black yarn.

Using the skin-coloured yarn, pull up 2 stitches just below the centre of the eyes and pull tightly to create the nose. Sew neatly inside the body so that no thread is visible.

Using pink yarn, make 2 stitches just below the nose to create the mouth. You can give the doll different facial expressions by where you choose to place the mouth.

Runner's outfit

Vest

Cut 2 vest shapes using the template on the following page. Sew both side seams using a neat running stitch.

Sew the front right shoulder strap to the back shoulder strap directly behind it. Repeat on the left side. Turn the vest inside out so that no seams show on the outside.

Sew all edges under by 0.5cm (¼in) using a neat running stitch in a contrasting coloured thread. This adds a little detail to an otherwise plain vest.

Number

Print a number onto paper using your computer (you can write it if you prefer) and cut round it in a square.

Attach it to the vest by making small stitches in each corner.

Shorts

Cut 4 shorts shapes using the template on the following page.

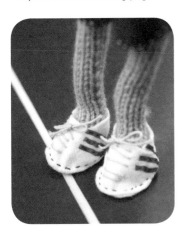

Sew the bottom and side edges under using a neat running stitch in a contrasting coloured thread. Repeat on all 4 sides.

Place the front left leg piece on top of the corresponding back leg piece and repeat with the right leg pieces.

Sew both inside seams using a neat running stitch to join the front leg pieces to the corresponding back leg pieces.

Sew the front seam to join the 2 front pieces together, then repeat to join the back pieces. Ensure the seams are on the inside.

Overlap the front side on the back side by about 1cm (½in) and pin it in place. Repeat for the other side. This creates the overlapped look that running shorts have.

Sew around the top of the shorts using a neat running stitch to neaten the edge, ensuring the folded down edge is on the inside.

Shoes

Cut 2 shoe backs, 2 soles and 2 shoe fronts using the templates on the following pages.

Sew the bottom of the 2 shoe backs to the back edge of both soles using a neat running stitch in contrasting thread. Wrap the front pieces around the front sections of the sole and sew it securely.

Cut up 6 small pieces of ribbon for each shoe.

Sew 3 to each side to add detail. This also attaches the front section of the shoe to the back making it less likely to fall off.

Thread a sharp needle with white yarn and stitch up the front of the shoe to give the appearance of laces. Tie with a bow at the top.

Reg the Runner Templates

Vest x 2

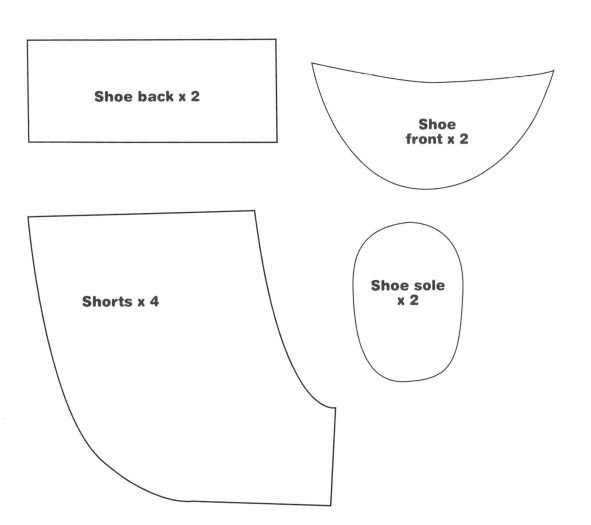

Shoe back x 2

Shoe front x 2

Shorts x 4

Shoe sole x 2

Wayne the Weightlifter

Needles

4mm (US size 6) knitting needles

Yarn

50g (2oz) oatmeal DK (this will make 2 dolls)
Oddments of light brown yarn for hair, brown or black for eyes and pink for mouth

Other materials

Aqua t-shirt fabric for vest (an old t-shirt works very well for this)
Contrasting coloured thread for vest
Blue t-shirt fabric for trousers
Brown felt for shoes

Dark thread for shoes
Brown felt or leather for belt
Grey felt for buckle

Gauge

22sts and 30 rows to 10cm (4in)

NOTE ON GAUGE

All knitters have slightly different gauge, so it's important to check your gauge so that the outfit your athlete will wear fits properly. If you have more than the stated sts/rows to your 10cm (4in) swatch, then use slightly larger needles. If fewer, use slightly smaller needles.

Finished size

Approximately 33cm (13in) tall.

Abbreviations

K2tog knit the next 2 stitches together
Kfb knit forward and back into the same stitch to make 2 stitches
P2tog purl the next 2 stitches together
Rep repeat
Skpo slip 1, knit 1, pass the slipped stitch over the knitted stitch

Pattern

Head, body and legs

Start at top of head.
Cast on 7 sts.
Row 1 [Kfb] 6 times, k1 (13 sts).
Row 2 P.
Row 3 [Kfb, k1, kfb] 4 times, k1 (21 sts).
Row 4 P.
Row 5 [Kfb, k3, kfb] 4 times, k1 (29 sts).
Row 6 P.
Row 7 K6, [kfb] 2 times, k12, [kfb] 2 times, k7 (33 sts).
Row 8 P.
Rows 9–22 Stocking/stockinette stitch.
Row 23 K6, skpo, k2tog, k12, skpo, k2tog, k7 (29 sts).
Row 24 P.

Row 25 [K2tog, k3, skpo] 4 times, k1 (21 sts).
Row 26 P.
Row 27 K.
Row 28 P.
Body
Row 29 [Kfb] rep in all sts (42 sts).
Row 30 P.
Rows 31–54 Stocking/stockinette stitch.
Row 55 [K1, k2tog] rep to end of row (28 sts).
Row 56 P.
Legs
Row 57 K14, turn (hold left leg sts and continue on 14 sts for right leg).
Row 58 P.
Row 59 K.
Row 60 P.
Row 61 K6, [kfb] 2 times, k6 (16 sts).
Row 62 P.
Row 63 K7, [kfb] 2 times, k7 (18 sts).
Row 64 P.
Rows 65–70 Stocking/stockinette stitch.
Row 71 K7, skpo, k2tog, k7 (16 sts).
Row 72 P.
Row 73 K6, skpo, k2tog, k6 (14 sts).
Row 74 P.
Rows 75–76 Stocking/stockinette stitch.
Row 77 K6, [kfb] 2 times, k6 (16 sts).
Row 78 P.
Rows 79–82 Stocking/stockinette stitch.
Row 83 K6, skpo, k2tog, k6 (14 sts).
Row 84 P.
Row 85 K5, skpo, k2tog, k5 (12 sts).
Row 86 P.
Feet
Row 87 K5, [kfb] 2 times, k5 (14 sts).
Row 88 P.
Row 89 K6, [kfb] 2 times, k6 (16 sts).
Row 90 P.
Row 91 K7, [kfb] 2 times, k7 (18 sts).
Row 92 P2tog, p14, p2tog (16 sts).
Row 93 K2tog, k12, k2tog (14 sts).
Row 94 [P2tog] rep to end of row (7 sts).
Thread yarn through remaining sts. Rep on remaining 14 sts for left leg.

Arms (make 2)
Cast on 14 sts.
Rows 1–4 Stocking/stockinette stitch.
Row 5 K6, [kfb] 2 times, k6 (16 sts).

Row 6 P.
Row 7 K7, [kfb] 2 times, k7 (18 sts).
Row 8 P.
Rows 9–12 Stocking/stockinette stitch.
Row 13 K7, skpo, k2tog, k7 (16 sts).
Row 14 P.
Row 15 K6, skpo, k2tog, k6 (14 sts).
Row 16 P.

Rows 17–18 Stocking/stockinette stitch.
Row 19 K6, [kfb] 2 times, k6 (16 sts).
Row 20 P.
Rows 21–22 Stocking/stockinette stitch.
Row 23 K6, skpo, k2tog, k6 (14 sts).
Row 24 P.
Row 25 K5, skpo, k2tog, k5 (12 sts).
Row 26 P.
Hands
Row 27 K2, [kfb] 2 times, k3, [kfb] 2 times, k3 (16 sts).
Row 28 P.
Rows 29–36 Stocking/stockinette stitch.
Row 37 [K2tog] rep to end of row (8 sts).
Thread yarn through remaining sts.

Making up
Head, body and legs
The head, body and legs are knitted all in one.
Sew down the back of the body and head and fill with stuffing. Sew down the back of the legs to the tips of the toes. Fill with stuffing as you go as the legs are thin.
Arms
Sew up the arm seams, filling with stuffing as you go.
Sew the arms on to the body using the neck shaping to help with positioning.
Hair
Sew short pieces of brown yarn to the head. Unravel the yarn to create the appearance of spiky hair.
Facial features
Embroider eyes using brown or black yarn.
Using the skin-coloured yarn, pull up 2 stitches just below the centre of the eyes and pull tightly to create the nose. Sew neatly inside the body so that no thread is visible.
Using pink yarn, make 2 stitches just below the nose to create the mouth. You can give the doll different facial expressions by where you choose to place the mouth.

Weightlifter's outfit
Vest
Cut 2 vest shapes using the template on the following page.
Sew both side seams using a neat running stitch.
Sew the front right shoulder strap to the back shoulder strap directly behind it. Repeat on the left side.
Turn the vest inside out so that no seams show on outside.
Sew all edges under by 0.5cm (¼in) using a neat running stitch in a contrasting coloured thread. This adds a little detail to an otherwise plain vest.
Trousers
Cut 4 trouser shapes using the template on the following page.
Place the front left leg piece on top of the corresponding back leg piece and repeat with the right leg pieces.
Sew both outside seams using a neat running stitch to join the front leg pieces to the corresponding back leg pieces.
Sew both inside seams using a neat running stitch.
Sew the front seam to join the 2 front pieces together, then repeat to join the back pieces.
Turn the trousers right side out and sew around the top of the trousers using a neat running stitch to neaten the edge, ensuring the folded down edge is on the inside.
Shoes
Cut 2 shoe backs, 2 soles and 2 shoe fronts using the templates on the following page.
Sew the bottom of the 2 shoe backs to the back edge of both soles using a neat running stitch. (The longer ankle section will wrap

round the leg and create the boot.)
Sew the bottom of the 2 shoe
fronts to the front edge of the
soles.
Sew the sides of the shoe backs
together at the front of the shoe
using cross-stitch and working
from bottom to top to enclose the
shoe around the ankle. Tie the
ends of the thread in a bow.

Belt

Cut a belt from brown felt or
leather and wrap a round the waist
of the doll.
Cut a belt buckle from grey felt
using the template on the following
page and thread the belt through
the buckle hole.
Secure using knot stitches to keep
the belt in place and add detail.

Wayne the Weightlifter Templates

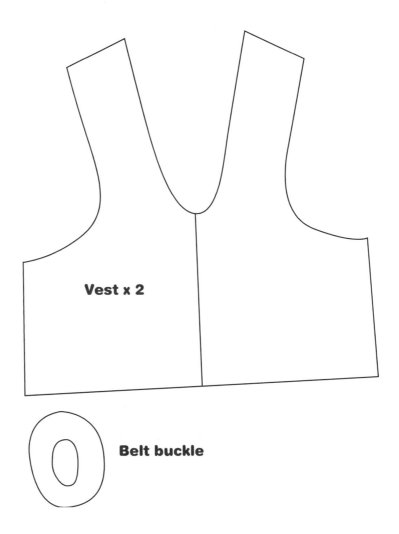

Vest x 2

Belt buckle

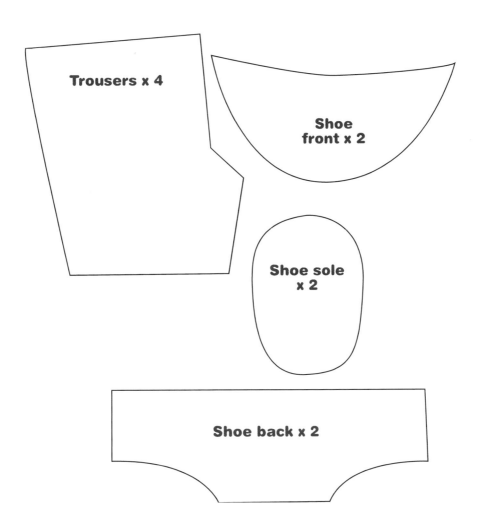

Trousers x 4

Shoe
front x 2

Shoe sole
x 2

Shoe back x 2

Gloria the Gymnast

Needles

4mm (US size 6) knitting needles

Yarn

50g (2oz) taupe DK (this will make 2 dolls)
Oddments of brown yarn for hair,

brown or black for eyes and pink for mouth

Other materials

Stuffing
Gold stretchy fabric for the leotard (any fabric with lycra will work,

old swimming costumes are particularly good)
Sequins for the leotard
Sequin strip for hair decoration

Gauge

22sts and 30 rows to 10cm (4in)

NOTE ON GAUGE

All knitters have slightly different gauge, so it's important to check your gauge so that the outfit your athlete will wear fits properly. If you have more than the stated sts/rows to your 10cm (4in) swatch, then use slightly larger needles. If fewer, use slightly smaller needles.

Finished size

Approximately 33cm (13in) tall.

Abbreviations

K2tog knit the next 2 stitches together
Kfb knit forward and back into the same stitch to make 2 stitches
P2tog purl the next 2 stitches together
Rep repeat
Skpo slip 1, knit 1, pass the slipped stitch over the knitted stitch

Pattern

Head, body and legs

Start at top of head.

Cast on 7 sts.

Row 1 [Kfb] 6 times, k1 (13 sts).

Row 2 P.

Row 3 [Kfb, k1, kfb] 4 times, k1 (21 sts).

Row 4 P.

Row 5 [Kfb, k3, kfb] 4 times, k1 (29 sts).

Row 6 P.

Row 7 K6, [kfb] 2 times, k12, [kfb] 2 times, k7 (33 sts).

Row 8 P.

Rows 9–22 Stocking/stockinette stitch.

Row 23 K6, skpo, k2tog, k12, skpo, k2tog, k7 (29 sts).

Row 24 P.

Row 25 [K2tog, k3, skpo] 4 times, k1 (21 sts).

Row 26 P.

Row 27 K.

Row 28 P.

Body

Row 29 [Kfb, k1] rep to last st, [kfb] (32 sts).

Row 30 P.

Rows 31–54 Stocking/stockinette stitch.

Row 55 [K2tog, k1] rep to last 2 sts, k2tog (21 sts).

Row 56 P.

Legs

Row 57 K9, k2tog, turn (hold left leg sts and continue on 10 sts for right leg).

Row 58 P.

Rows 59–88 Stocking/stockinette stitch.

Feet

Row 89 K4, [kfb] 2 times, k4 (12 sts).

Row 90 P.

Row 91 K5, [kfb] 2 times, k5 (14 sts).

Row 92 P.

Row 93 K6, [kfb] 2 times, k6 (16 sts).

Row 94 P2tog, p12, p2tog (14 sts).

Row 95 K2tog, k10, k2tog (12 sts).

Row 96 [P2tog] rep to end of row (6 sts).

Thread yarn through remaining sts.

Rep on remaining 10 sts for left leg.

Sew down the back of the body and head and fill with stuffing.
Sew down the inner legs to the tips of the toes. Fill with stuffing as you go as the legs are thin.

Arms

Sew up the arm seams, filling with stuffing as you go.
Sew the arms on to the body using the neck shaping to help with positioning.

Hair

Wrap the yarn around a large book (the book I used was about 27cm/10¾in tall). The bigger the book, the longer the hair.
Continue wrapping the yarn round the book until it is approximately 4cm (1½in) wide and 0.5–1cm (¼–½in) thick. The more yarn you wrap, the thicker the hair.
Carefully stitch over and under one side of the hair then back again so that every strand of hair is captured in the stitches.
Cut the hair on the other side of the book so that there is an even amount of hair each side of the stitches.
Position the hair at the top of the head with the stitches in the centre. Spread the hair so that it runs down the side and back of the doll's head.
Sew the hair tightly along the top

Arms (make 2)

Cast on 10 sts.
Rows 1–30 Stocking/stockinette stitch.

Hands

Row 31 K1, [kfb] 2 times, k3, [kfb] 2 times, k2 (14 sts).
Row 32 P.
Rows 33–36 Stocking/stockinette stitch.
Row 37 [K2tog] rep to end of row (7 sts).
Thread yarn through remaining sts.

Making up
Head, body and legs

The head, body and legs are knitted all in one.

of her head and round the bottom, back and sides of the head. Every strand of hair needs to be sewn down.

Facial features

Embroider eyes using brown or black yarn.

Using the skin-coloured yarn, pull up 2 stitches just below the centre of the eyes and pull tightly to create the nose. Sew neatly inside the body so that no thread is visible.

Using pink yarn, make 2 stitches just below the nose to create the mouth. You can give the doll different facial expressions by where you choose to place the mouth.

Gymnast's outfit
Leotard

Fold the fabric in half and pin the template on the following page to it with the base on the fold line. Cut around the edge of the template, remembering not to cut along the fold line. Sew both side seams using a neat running stitch. Sew the front right shoulder strap to the back shoulder strap directly behind it. Repeat for the left side.

Turn the costume right side out so that no seams show.

Carefully stitch a string of sequins around the edges of the legs, neck and arms.

Hair decoration

To make the sequined clip and bun, fold the hair up onto the back of the head and slightly twist it. Sew it into place using the same yarn used to create the hair. Cut a 10cm (4in) length of the sequin strip and sew it over the hair stitches to give the impression of a clip.

Gloria the Gymnast Template

Costume

FOLD

Bill and Bob the Boxers

Needles

4mm (US size 6) knitting needles

Yarn

50g (2oz) skin coloured DK (this will make 2 dolls)

25g (1oz) or large oddment red DK for gloves

Oddments of brown or black and white for eyes and pink for mouth

Other materials

Stuffing

Shiny fabric for vest and shorts

Matching thread for vest and shorts

Contrasting fabric for short's waistband

Felt for shoes

Fine satin ribbon

Gauge

22sts and 30 rows to 10cm (4in)

NOTE ON GAUGE

All knitters have slightly different gauge, so it's important to check your gauge so that the outfit your athlete will wear fits properly. If you have more than the stated sts/rows to your 10cm (4in) swatch, then use slightly larger needles. If fewer, use slightly smaller needles.

Finished size

Approximately 33cm (13in) tall.

Abbreviations

K2tog knit the next 2 stitches together

Kfb knit forward and back into the same stitch to make 2 stitches

P2tog purl the next 2 stitches together

Rep repeat

Skpo slip 1, knit 1, pass the slipped stitch over the knitted stitch

Pattern

Head, body and legs

Start at top of head.

Cast on 7 sts.

Row 1 [Kfb] 6 times, k1 (13 sts).

Row 2 P.

Row 3 [Kfb, k1, kfb] 4 times, k1 (21 sts).

Row 4 P.

Row 5 [Kfb, k3, kfb] 4 times, k1 (29 sts).

Row 6 P.

Row 7 K6, [kfb] 2 times, k12, [kfb] 2 times, k7 (33 sts).

Row 8 P.

Rows 9–22 Stocking/stockinette stitch.

Row 23 K6, skpo, k2tog, k12, skpo, k2tog, k7 (29 sts).

Row 24 P.

Row 25 [K2tog, k3, skpo] 4 times, k1 (21 sts).

Row 26 P.

Row 27 K.

Row 28 P.

Body

Row 29 [Kfb] rep in all sts (42 sts).

Row 30 P.

Rows 31–54 Stocking/stockinette stitch.

Row 55 [K1, k2tog] rep to end of row (28 sts).

Row 56 P.

Legs

Row 57 K14, turn (hold left leg sts and continue on 14 sts for right leg).

Row 58 P.

Row 59 K.

Row 60 P.

Row 61 K6, [kfb] 2 times, k6 (16 sts).

Row 62 P.

Row 63 K7, [kfb] 2 times, k7 (18 sts).

Row 64 P.

Rows 65–70 Stocking/stockinette stitch.

Row 71 K7, skpo, k2tog, k7 (16 sts).

Row 72 P.

Row 73 K6, skpo, k2tog, k6 (14 sts).

Row 74 P.

Rows 75–76 Stocking/stockinette stitch.

Row 77 K6, [kfb] 2 times, k6 (16 sts).

Row 78 P.

Rows 79–82 Stocking/stockinette stitch.

Row 83 K6, skpo, k2tog, k6 (14 sts).

Row 84 P.

Row 85 K5, skpo, k2tog, k5 (12 sts).

Row 86 P.

Feet

Row 87 K5, [kfb] 2 times, k5 (14 sts).

Row 88 P.

Row 89 K6, [kfb] 2 times, k6 (16 sts).

Row 90 P.

Row 91 K7, [kfb] 2 times, k7 (18 sts).

Row 92 P2tog, p14, p2tog (16 sts).

Row 93 K2tog, k12, k2tog (14 sts).
Row 94 [P2tog] rep to end of row (7 sts).
Thread yarn through remaining sts. Rep on remaining 14 sts for left leg.

Arms (make 2)
Cast on 14 sts.
Rows 1–4 Stocking/stockinette stitch.
Row 5 K6, [kfb] 2 times, k6 (16 sts).
Row 6 P.
Row 7 K7, [kfb] 2 times, k7 (18 sts).
Row 8 P.
Rows 9–12 Stocking/stockinette stitch.
Row 13 K7, skpo, k2tog, k7 (16 sts).
Row 14 P.
Row 15 K6, skpo, k2tog, k6 (14 sts).
Row 16 P.
Rows 17–18 Stocking/stockinette stitch.
Row 19 K6, [kfb] 2 times, k6 (16 sts).
Row 20 P.
Rows 21–22 Stocking/stockinette stitch.
Row 23 K6, skpo, k2tog, k6 (14 sts).
Row 24 P.
Row 25 K5, skpo, k2tog, k5 (12 sts).
Row 26 P.
Hands
Row 27 K2, [kfb] 2 times, k3, [kfb] 2 times, k3 (16 sts).
Row 28 P.
Rows 29–36 Stocking/stockinette stitch.
Row 37 [K2tog] rep to end of row (8 sts).
Thread yarn through remaining sts.

Making up
Head, body and legs
The head, body and legs are knitted all in one.
Sew down the back of the body and head and fill with stuffing.
Sew down the back of the legs to the tips of the toes. Fill with stuffing as you go as the legs are thin.
Arms
Sew up the arm seams, filling with stuffing as you go.
Sew the arms on to the body using the neck shaping to help with positioning.
Facial features
Embroider eyes using brown or black yarn, highlighted with white yarn.
Using the skin-coloured yarn, pull up 2 stitches just below the centre

of the eyes and pull tightly to create the nose. Sew the pink yarn neatly inside the body so that no thread is visible.

Using pink yarn, make 2 stitches just below the nose to create the mouth. You can give the doll different facial expressions by where you choose to place the mouth.

Boxer's outfit

Vest

Cut 2 vest shapes using the template on the following page. Sew both side seams using a neat running stitch.

Sew the front right shoulder strap to the back shoulder strap directly behind it. Repeat on the left side. Turn the vest inside out so that no seams show on outside.

Sew all edges under by 0.5cm (¼in) using a neat running stitch, attaching a ribbon round the neck and arms at the same time. This adds a little detail to an otherwise plain vest.

Shorts

Cut 4 shorts shapes using the template on the following page. Place the front left leg piece on top of the corresponding back leg piece and repeat with the right leg pieces.

Sew both outside seams using a neat running stitch to join the front leg pieces to the corresponding back leg pieces.

Sew both inside seams using a neat running stitch.

Starting at the top, join 2 front and 2 back pieces together by sewing down the front seam, between the legs and up the back to the waist, ensuring the seams on the inside of the shorts.

Sew around the bottom of each shorts leg.

Cut out the waistband in a contrasting fabric using the template on the following page. Fold the fabric at the fold marks, wrap it around the waist of the shorts and sew it neatly to the top of the shorts. I sandwiched the top of the shorts inside the band to give a neater edge.

Shoes

Cut 2 shoe backs, 2 soles and 2 shoe fronts using the templates on the following page.

Sew the bottom of the 2 shoe backs to the back edge of both soles using a neat running stitch. (The longer ankle section will wrap round the leg and create the boot.)

Sew the bottom of the 2 shoe fronts to the front edge of the soles.

Sew the sides of the shoe backs together at the front of the shoe using cross-stitch in a fine satin ribbon and working from bottom to top to enclose the shoe around the ankle. Tie the ends of the ribbon in a bow.

Gloves (make 2)

Cast on 15 sts with red yarn.

Rows 1–4 K.

Row 5 P.

Row 6 K3, [kfb] 2 times, k4, [kfb] 2 times, k4 (19 sts).

Row 7 P.

Rows 8–15 Stocking/stockinette stitch.

Row 16 [K2tog] rep to last st, k1. Thread yarn through stitches.

Bob the Boxer Templates

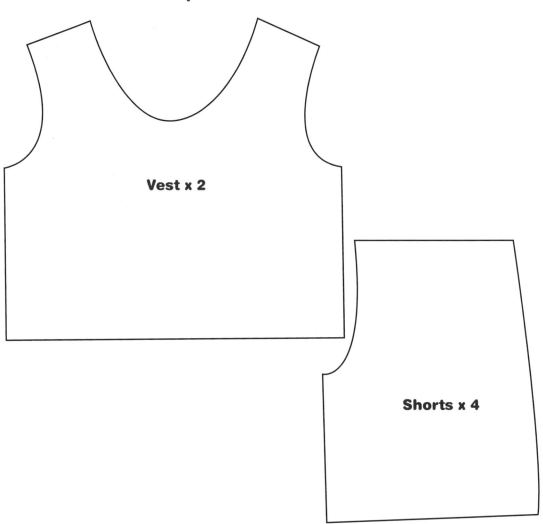

Vest x 2

Shorts x 4

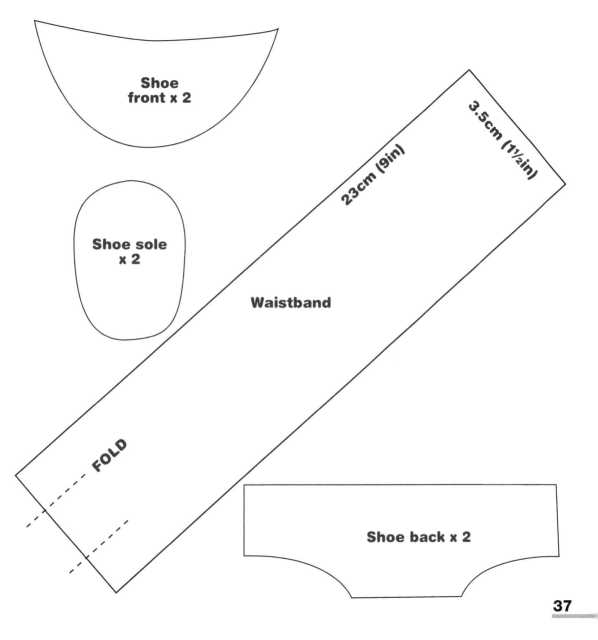

Shoe front x 2

Shoe sole x 2

3.5cm (1½in)

23cm (9in)

Waistband

FOLD

Shoe back x 2

Cindy the Cyclist

Needles

4mm (US size 6) knitting needles

Yarn

50g (2oz) oatmeal DK (this will make 2 dolls)
Oddments of brown yarn for hair, brown or black for eyes and pink for mouth

Other materials

Stuffing
Lycra fabric for vest and a contrasting coloured fabric for sleeves, shorts and shoes (old swimming costumes or cycling shorts work well)
Matching thread for vest, shorts and shorts
Blue and white felt for helmet
Matching thread for helmet

Gauge

22sts and 30 rows to 10cm (4in)

NOTE ON GAUGE

All knitters have slightly different gauge, so it's important to check your gauge so that the outfit your athlete will wear fits properly. If you have more than the stated sts/rows to your 10cm (4in) swatch, then use slightly larger needles. If fewer, use slightly smaller needles.

Finished size

Approximately 33cm (13in) tall.

Abbreviations

K2tog knit the next 2 stitches together
Kfb knit forward and back into the same stitch to make 2 stitches
P2tog purl the next 2 stitches together
Rep repeat
Skpo slip 1, knit 1, pass the slipped stitch over the knitted stitch

Pattern

Head, body and legs

Start at top of head.
Cast on 7 sts.

Row 1 [Kfb] 6 times, k1 (13 sts).
Row 2 P.
Row 3 [Kfb, k1, kfb] 4 times, k1 (21 sts).
Row 4 P.
Row 5 [Kfb, k3, kfb] 4 times, k1 (29 sts).
Row 6 P.
Row 7 K6, [kfb] 2 times, k12, [kfb] 2 times, k7 (33 sts).
Row 8 P.
Rows 9–22 Stocking/stockinette stitch.
Row 23 K6, skpo, k2tog, k12, skpo, k2tog, k7 (29 sts).
Row 24 P.
Row 25 [K2tog, k3, skpo] 4 times, k1 (21 sts).
Row 26 P.

Row 27 K.

Row 28 P.

Body

Row 29 [Kfb, k1] rep to last st, [kfb] (32 sts).

Row 30 P.

Rows 31–54 Stocking/stockinette stitch.

Row 55 [K2tog, k1] rep to last 2 sts, k2tog (21 sts).

Row 56 P.

Legs

Row 57 K9, k2tog, turn (hold left leg sts and continue on 10 sts for right leg).

Row 58 P.

Rows 59–88 Stocking/stockinette stitch.

Feet

Row 89 K4, [kfb] 2 times, k4 (12 sts).

Row 90 P.

Row 91 K5, [kfb] 2 times, k5 (14 sts).

Row 92 P.

Row 93 K6, [kfb] 2 times, k6 (16 sts).

Row 94 P2tog, p12, p2tog (14 sts).

Row 95 K2tog, k10, k2tog (12 sts).

Row 96 [P2tog] rep to end of row (6 sts).

Thread yarn through remaining sts. Rep on remaining 10 sts for left leg.

Arms (make 2)

Cast on 10 sts.

Rows 1–30 Stocking/stockinette stitch.

Hands

Row 31 K1, [kfb] 2 times, k3, [kfb] 2 times, k2 (14 sts).

Row 32 P.

Rows 33–36 Stocking/stockinette stitch.

Row 37 [K2tog] rep to end of row (7 sts).

Thread yarn through remaining sts.

Making up
Head, body and legs

The head, body and legs are knitted all in one.

Sew down the back of the body and head and fill with stuffing.

Sew down the inner legs to the tips of the toes. Fill with stuffing as you go as the legs are thin.

Arms

Sew up the arm seams, filling with stuffing as you go.

Sew the arms on to the body using the neck shaping to help with positioning

Facial features

Embroider eyes using brown or black yarn.

Using the skin-coloured yarn, pull up 2 stitches just below the centre of the eyes and pull tightly to create the nose. Sew neatly inside the body so that no thread is visible.

Using pink yarn, make 2 stitches just below the nose to create the mouth. You can give the doll different facial expressions by where you choose to place the mouth.

Cyclist's outfit
Vest

Cut 2 vest shapes using the template on the following page. Sew both side seams using a neat running stitch.

Sew the vest together at the shoulders.

Cut 2 sleeves using the template on the following page.

Sew the bottom of each sleeve using a neat running stitch to give a neat edge.

Fold both sleeves in half along the fold line with the right sides together and sew to the under arm. Turn the sleeves in the right way so that the seams are on the inside.

Slip them in the hole of the arm so that the arm seam is in line with the side of the top seam.

Sew the opening of the sleeve round the arm hole. Repeat for the second arm. All the stitches should

be in the inside so that they can't be seen on the outside.

Turn the vest right side out so the seams are on the inside.

Sew around the edges of the neck using a neat running stitch to give a neat finish.

Shorts

Cut 4 shorts shapes using the template on the following page. Place the front left leg piece on top of the corresponding back leg piece and repeat with the right leg pieces.

Sew both outside seams using a neat running stitch to join the front leg pieces to the corresponding back leg pieces.

Sew both inside seams using a neat running stitch.

Starting at the top, join 2 front and 2 back pieces together by sewing down the front seam, between the legs and up the back to the waist, ensuring the seams are on the inside of the shorts.

Sew neatly around the waist of the shorts and the bottom of each leg, ensuring the folded down edge is on the inside.

Shoes

Cut 2 shoe shapes using the template on the following page. Fold in half and sew the curved outside edges together using a neat running stitch.

Turn the shoes the ride side out and place them onto the feet of the doll.

Helmet

Cut a helmet shape using the template on the following page. Fold in half, cut out the holes and sew the curved outside edges together using a neat running stitch.

Cut the under chin strap and sew to the front of the hat.

Cut 4 narrow strips of white felt. Sew 1 around the base of the helmet, sew another over the top and the final 2 pieces around the sides.

Cut the visor and sew to the front of the helmet.

Cindy the Cyclist Templates

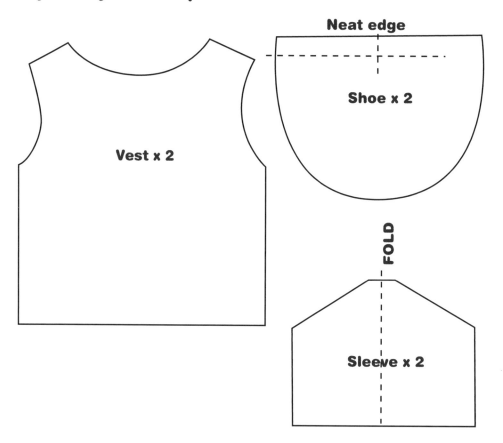

Vest x 2

Neat edge

Shoe x 2

FOLD

Sleeve x 2

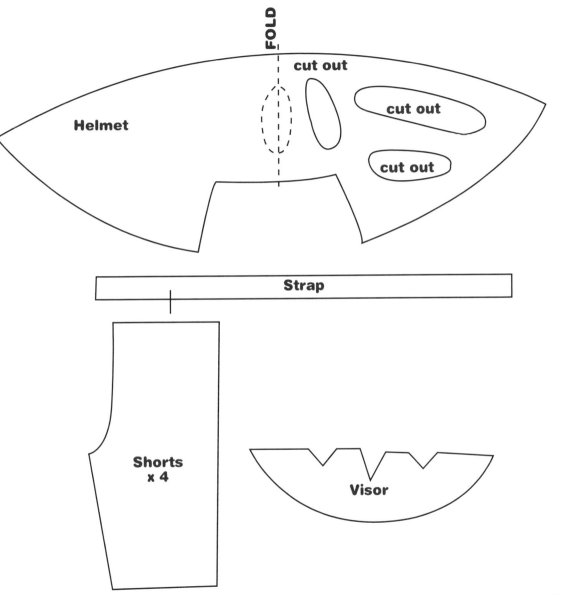

FOLD

cut out

cut out

cut out

Helmet

Strap

Shorts
x 4

Visor

Fiona the Fencer

Needles

4mm (US size 6) knitting needles

Yarn

50g (2oz) oatmeal DK (this will make 2 dolls)

Oddments of brown for hair, brown or black for eyes and pink for mouth

Other materials

Stuffing

White t-shirt fabric for leggings, sleeves and face mask strip (an old t-shirt works very well for this)

Matching thread for leggings and sleeves

Jersey fabric for protective vest and gloves

Matching thread for protective vest and gloves

Black netting for facemask

White felt for facemask and shoes

Contrasting thread for shoes

Grey ribbon for headband and glove

Gauge

22sts and 30 rows to 10cm (4in)

NOTE ON GAUGE

All knitters have slightly different gauge, so it's important to check your gauge so that the outfit your athlete will wear fits properly. If you

have more than the stated sts/rows to your 10cm (4in) swatch, then use slightly larger needles. If fewer, use slightly smaller needles.

Finished size

Approximately 33cm (13in) tall.

Abbreviations

K2tog knit the next 2 stitches together

Kfb knit forward and back into the

same stitch to make 2 stitches

P2tog purl the next 2 stitches together

Rep repeat

Skpo slip 1, knit 1, pass the slipped stitch over the knitted stitch

Pattern

Head, body and legs

Start at top of head.

Cast on 7 sts.

Row 1 [Kfb] 6 times, k1 (13 sts).
Row 2 P.
Row 3 [Kfb, k1, kfb] 4 times, k1 (21 sts).
Row 4 P.
Row 5 [Kfb, k3, kfb] 4 times, k1 (29 sts).
Row 6 P.
Row 7 K6, [kfb] 2 times, k12, [kfb] 2 times, k7 (33 sts).
Row 8 P.
Rows 9–22 Stocking/stockinette stitch.

Row 23 K6, skpo, k2tog, k12, skpo, k2tog, k7 (29 sts).
Row 24 P.
Row 25 [K2tog, k3, skpo] 4 times, k1 (21 sts).
Row 26 P.
Row 27 K.
Row 28 P.
Body
Row 29 [Kfb, k1] rep to last st, [kfb] (32 sts).

Row 30 P.
Rows 31–54 Stocking/stockinette stitch.
Row 55 [K2tog, k1] rep to last 2 sts, k2tog (21 sts).
Row 56 P.
Legs
Row 57 K9, k2tog, turn (hold left leg sts and continue on 10 sts for right leg).
Row 58 P.
Rows 59–88 Stocking/stockinette stitch.
Feet
Row 89 K4, [kfb] 2 times, k4 (12 sts).
Row 90 P.
Row 91 K5, [kfb] 2 times, k5 (14 sts).
Row 92 P.
Row 93 K6, [kfb] 2 times, k6 (16 sts).
Row 94 P2tog, p12, p2tog (14 sts).
Row 95 K2tog, k10, k2tog (12 sts).
Row 96 [P2tog] rep to end of row (6 sts).
Thread yarn through remaining sts. Rep on remaining 10 sts for left leg.

Arms (make 2)
Cast on 10 sts.
Rows 1–30 Stocking/stockinette stitch.
Hands

Row 31 K1, [kfb] 2 times, k3, [kfb] 2 times, k2 (14 sts).
Row 32 P.
Rows 33–36 Stocking/stockinette stitch.
Row 37 [K2tog] rep to end of row (7 sts).
Thread yarn through remaining sts.

Making up
Head, body and legs
The head, body and legs are knitted all in one.
Sew down the back of the body and head and fill with stuffing.
Sew down the inner legs to the tips of the toes. Fill with stuffing as you go as the legs are thin.

Arms
Sew up the arm seams, filling with stuffing as you go.
Sew the arms on to the body using the neck shaping to help with positioning

Hair
Wrap the yarn around a large book (the book I used was about 27cm/10¾in tall). The bigger the book, the longer the hair.
Continue wrapping the yarn round the book until it is approximately 4cm (1½in) wide and 0.5 –1cm (¼–½in) thick. The more yarn you wrap, the thicker the hair.
Carefully stitch over and under one side of the hair then back again so that every strand of hair is captured in the stitches.
Cut the hair on the other side of the book so that there is an even amount of hair each side of the stitches.
Position the hair at the top of the head with the stitches in the centre. Spread the hair so that it runs down the side and back of the doll's head.
Sew the hair tightly along the top of her head and round the bottom, back and sides of the head. Every strand of hair needs to be sewn down.

Facial features
Embroider eyes using brown or black yarn.
Using the skin-coloured yarn, pull up 2 stitches just below the centre of the eyes and pull tightly to create the nose. Sew neatly inside the body so that no thread is visible.
Using pink yarn, make 2 stitches just below the nose to create the mouth. You can give the doll different facial expressions by where you choose to place the mouth.

Fencer's outfit
Leggings
Cut 4 legging shapes using the template on the following pages.
Place the front left leg piece on top of the corresponding back leg piece and repeat with the right leg pieces.
Sew both outside seams using a neat running stitch to join the front leg pieces to the corresponding back leg pieces.
Sew both inside seams using a neat running stitch.
Starting at the top, join 2 front and 2 back pieces together by sewing down the front seam, between the

legs and up the back to the waist, ensuring the seams on the inside of the leggings.

Sew neatly around the waist of the leggings and the bottom of each leg, ensuring the folded down edge is on the inside.

Protective vest

To cut the vest shape, fold the fabric in half and pin the template on the following page to it with the fold of the fabric at the base of the template.

Cut around the edge of the template remembering not to cut along the base fold line.

Sew both side seams using a neat running stitch.

Sew the vest together at the shoulders.

Turn the vest right side out so the seams are on the inside.

Sew around the edges of the legs, neck and arms using a neat running stitch to give a neat finish.

Sleeves

Cut 2 sleeve shapes using the template on the following page.

Sew the bottom of each sleeve using a neat running stitch to give a neat edge.

Fold both sleeves in half with the right sides together and stitch from the cuff to under the arm.

Turn the sleeves the right side out

so the seams are on the inside. Slip the sleeves into the vest arm holes so that the arm seams are in line with the side of the vest seam. Sew the opening of the sleeve around the arm hole ensuring the seam it on the inside. Repeat for the second arm.

Facemask

Cut out the facemask in black netting using the template on the following page.

Using the same t-shirt material you used for the leggings and the sleeves, cut out the strip and sew it around the top edge of the mask. This will help the mask to stay on the doll's head.

Cut out the back of head mask using the template on the following page and sew it to the strip on top of the mask.

Put the mask on the doll and wrap the grey ribbon for a headband around the back of the head. Cut and sew to fit.

Glove

Cut a glove shape in white jersey fabric.

Sew the outside edges together using a neat running stitch, remembering to leave an opening for the hand.

Turn the glove right side out. Trim with ribbon.

Shoes

Cut 2 shoe backs, 2 soles and 2 shoe fronts in white felt using the templates on the following page.

Sew the bottom of the 2 shoe backs to the back edge of both soles using a neat running stitch.

Wrap the front pieces around the front sections of the sole and sew in place.

Fiona the Fencer Templates

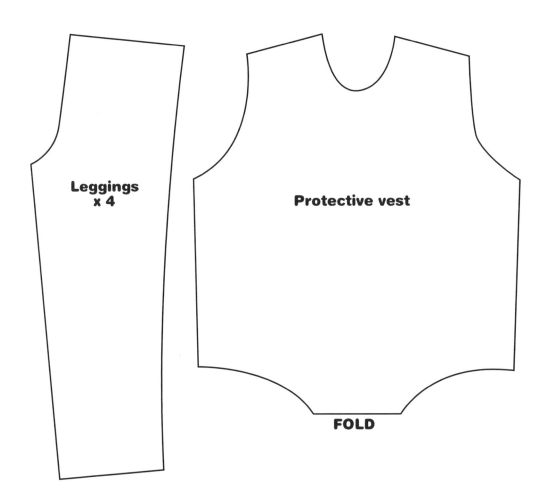

Leggings
x 4

Protective vest

FOLD

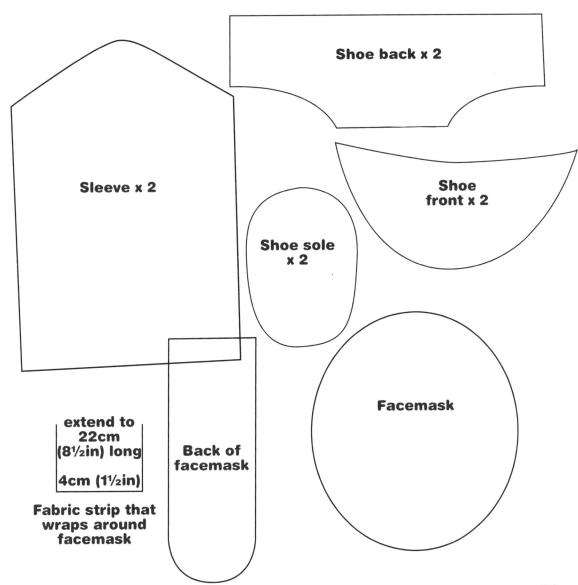

Sleeve x 2

Shoe back x 2

Shoe front x 2

Shoe sole x 2

Facemask

extend to 22cm (8½in) long

4cm (1½in)

Fabric strip that wraps around facemask

Back of facemask

Edward the Equestrian

Needles

4mm (US size 6) knitting needles

Yarn

50g (2oz) oatmeal DK (this will make 2 dolls)
Oddments of brown yarn for hair and moustache, brown or black for eyes and pink for mouth

Other materials

Stuffing
White t-shirt fabric for trousers (an old t-shirt works very well for this)
Red ribbon for trousers
Navy fabric for jacket
Gold thread for jacket and boots
White cotton fabric for shirt (an old shirt or sheet works well for this)

Black felt for boots
Black felt for hat

Gauge

22sts and 30 rows to 10cm (4in)

NOTE ON GAUGE

All knitters have slightly different gauge, so it's important to check your gauge so that the outfit your athlete will wear fits properly. If you have more than the stated sts/rows to your 10cm (4in) swatch, then use slightly larger needles. If fewer, use slightly smaller needles.

Finished size

Approximately 33cm (13in) tall.

Abbreviations

K2tog knit the next 2 stitches together
Kfb knit forward and back into the same stitch to make 2 stitches
P2tog purl the next 2 stitches together
Rep repeat
Skpo slip 1, knit 1, pass the slipped stitch over the knitted stitch

Pattern

Head, body and legs

Start at top of head.
Cast on 7 sts.
Row 1 [Kfb] 6 times, k1 (13 sts).
Row 2 P.
Row 3 [Kfb, k1, kfb] 4 times, k1 (21 sts).
Row 4 P.
Row 5 [Kfb, k3, kfb] 4 times, k1 (29 sts).
Row 6 P.
Row 7 K6, [kfb] 2 times, k12, [kfb] 2 times, k7 (33 sts).
Row 8 P.
Rows 9–22 Stocking/stockinette stitch.
Row 23 K6, skpo, k2tog, k12, skpo, k2tog, k7 (29 sts).
Row 24 P.
Row 25 [K2tog, k3, skpo] 4 times, k1 (21 sts).
Row 26 P.

Row 27 K.
Row 28 P.
Body
Row 29 [Kfb, k1] rep to last st, [kfb] (32 sts).
Row 30 P.
Rows 31–54 Stocking/stockinette stitch.
Row 55 [K2tog, k1] rep to last 2 sts, k2tog (21 sts).
Row 56 P.
Legs
Row 57 K9, k2tog, turn (hold left leg sts and continue on 10 sts for right leg).
Row 58 P.
Rows 59–88 Stocking/stockinette stitch.
Feet
Row 89 K4, [kfb] 2 times, k4 (12 sts).
Row 90 P.
Row 91 K5, [kfb] 2 times, k5 (14 sts).
Row 92 P.
Row 93 K6, [kfb] 2 times, k6 (16 sts).
Row 94 P2tog, p12, p2tog (14 sts).
Row 95 K2tog, k10, k2tog (12 sts).
Row 96 [P2tog] rep to end of row (6 sts).
Thread yarn through remaining sts.
Rep on remaining 10 sts for left leg.

Arms (make 2)
Cast on 10 sts.
Rows 1–30 Stocking/stockinette stitch.
Hands
Row 31 K1, [kfb] 2 times, k3, [kfb] 2 times, k2 (14 sts).
Row 32 P.
Rows 33–36 Stocking/stockinette stitch.
Row 37 [K2tog] rep to end of row (7 sts).
Thread yarn through remaining sts.

Making up
Head, body and legs
The head, body and legs are knitted all in one.
Sew down the back of the body and head and fill with stuffing.
Sew down the inner legs to the tips of the toes. Fill with stuffing as you go as the legs are thin.
Arms
Sew up the arm seams, filling with stuffing as you go.
Sew the arms on to the body using the neck shaping to help with positioning
Hair
Thread a long length of yarn into a thick needle (I used 2 lengths of yarn to make it quicker).
Sew 1cm (½in) stitches around the edge of the head to form the shape

of the hairline. Try to work the stitches in the direction that real hair takes.
Fill in the gaps with more stitches until the whole head of hair is covered.
Facial features
Embroider eyes using brown or black yarn.
Using the skin-coloured yarn, pull up 2 stitches just below the centre of the eyes and pull tightly to create the nose. Sew neatly inside the body so that no thread is visible.
Using pink yarn, make 2 stitches just below the nose to create the mouth. You can give the doll different facial expressions by where you choose to place the mouth.

Moustache

Cut 2 small strands of brown yarn and sew to the face under the nose.

Divide the strands of yarn to create the desired look.

Equestrian outfit
Trousers

Cut 4 trouser shapes using the template on the following page. Place the front left leg piece on top of the corresponding back leg piece and repeat with the right leg pieces.

Sew both outside seams using a neat running stitch to join the front leg pieces to the corresponding back leg pieces.

Sew both inside seams using a neat running stitch.

Starting at the top, join 2 front and 2 back pieces together by sewing down the front seam, between the legs and up the back to the waist, ensuring the seams on the inside of the trousers.

Sew neatly around the bottom of each leg, ensuring the folded down edge is on the inside.

Sew a length of red ribbon neatly around the top of the trousers.

Shirt

Cut out 2 shirt shapes in white cotton fabric using the template on the following pages.

Sew both side seams using a neat running stitch.

Sew the shirt together at the shoulders.

Turn the shirt right side out so the seams are on the inside.

Sew around all using a neat running stitch to give a neat finish.

Cut out a collar using the template on the following pages. Fold the collar and sandwich the fabric at the top of the shirt between it (this will be easier to sew once the shirt is on the doll).

As the shirt is worn under the jacket, there is no real need to add sleeves. However, if you'd like to add sleeves cut 2 sleeve shapes in white cotton fabric using the jacket sleeves template on the following pages and make-up using the instructions given above. You may need to slightly ease the fabric into the arm hole to make them fit.

Jacket

Cut out 2 sleeves, 2 jacket fronts, 1 jacket back and 1 collar in navy fabric using the templates on the following pages.

Sew both jacket fronts to the back of the jacket. The front pieces are shorter so make sure you line up the 2 fronts with the under arm section. Sew up the shoulders.

Sew the bottom of each sleeve using a neat running stitch to give a neat edge.

Fold both sleeves in half with the right sides together and stitch from the cuff to the under arm of the jacket.

Turn the sleeves right side out so the seams are on the inside.
Slip the sleeves into the arm holes so that the arm seams are in line with the side of the jacket seam. Sew the opening of the sleeve around the arm hole ensuring the seam it on the inside. Repeat for the second arm.

Turn the jacket right side out so the seams are on the inside

Fold the collar and sandwich the fabric at the top of the jacket between it. Sew in place.

Sew all the way around the base of the jacket including the back slit to create the jacket tails.

Put the jacket on to the doll and sew it together with 6 little gold stitches for buttons.

Boots

Cut 2 boot backs, 2 soles and 2 boot fronts in black felt using the templates on the following pages.

Sew the bottom of the 2 boot backs to the back edge of both soles using a neat running stitch. (The longer ankle section will wrap round the leg and create the boot.) Wrap the front pieces round the front of the sole and sew in place.

Cut out a strip of black felt and wrap it round the top of the boot (it is easier to do this once the boot is on the doll).

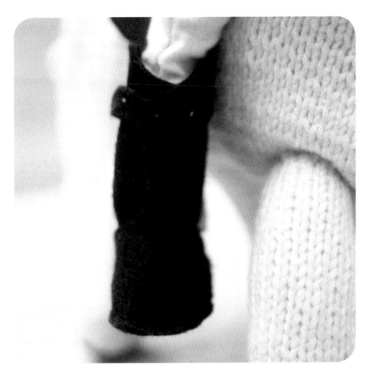

Embroider little gold stitches around the strap to give the impression of buttons.

Hat

Cut out the the base, rim and the top of the hat using the templates on the following pages. Remember to cut out the hole in the centre of the base so that the hat stays on the head. Make little snips all the way round the centre base so that

the hat can curve, as indicated on the template.

Sew both sides of the rim together to create a circular piece.

Slip it on top of the base and sew in place. Sew the top of the hat to the top of the rim.

Harry the Handsome Horse

Needles
4mm (US size 6) knitting needles

Yarn
50g (2oz) Rowan Calmer in shade 460
Oddments of brown or black yarn for hair, mane and eyes

Other materials
Stuffing

Card for mane (a cereal box works well)
Brown or black leather for saddle, stirrup strap and reins
Brown felt for saddle
Grey felt for stirrups and shoes

Gauge
22sts and 30 rows to 10cm (4in)

NOTE ON GAUGE
All knitters have slightly different gauge, so it's important to check your gauge so that the tack your horse will wear fits properly. If you have more than the stated sts/rows to your 10cm (4in) swatch, then use slightly larger needles. If fewer, use slightly smaller needles.

Finished size
Approximately 25cm (9¾in) long and 26cm (10¼in) tall

Abbreviations
K2tog knit the next 2 stitches together
Kfb knit forward and back into the same stitch to make 2 stitches
P2tog purl the next 2 stitches together
Rep repeat
Skpo slip 1, knit 1, pass the slipped stitch over the knitted stitch

Pattern
Head, neck and body
Start at nose.
Cast on 8 sts.
Row 1 [Kfb] rep to last st, k1

Row 1 [Kfb] rep to last st, k1 (15 sts).
Row 2 P.
Row 3 K4, kfb, k4, kfb, k5 (17 sts).
Row 4 P.
Row 5 K5, kfb, k4, kfb, k6 (19 sts).
Row 6 P.
Row 7 K6, kfb, k4, kfb, k7 (21 sts).
Row 8 P.
Row 9 K2, [kfb, k4] 3 times, kfb, k3 (25 sts).
Row 10 P.
Row 11 K2, kfb, k6, kfb, k4, kfb, k6, kfb, k3 (29 sts).
Row 12 P.
Row 13 K2, kfb, k8, kfb, k4, kfb, k8, kfb, k3 (33 sts).
Row 14 P.
Row 15 K2, kfb, k10, kfb, k4, kfb, k10, kfb, k3 (37 sts).
Row 16 P.
Row 17 K2, kfb, k12, kfb, k4, kfb, k12, kfb, k3 (41 sts).
Row 18 P.
Row 19 K2, kfb, k14, kfb, k4, kfb, k14, kfb, k3 (45 sts).
Row 20 P.
Row 21 K2, kfb, k16, kfb, k4, kfb, k16, kfb, k3 (49 sts).
Row 22 P.
Row 23 K.
Row 24 P.
Row 25 K.
Row 26 P.
Row 27 K2, skpo, k16, skpo, k5,

k2tog, k16, k2tog, k2 (45 sts).
Row 28 P.
Row 29 K2, skpo, k14, skpo, k5, k2tog, k14, k2tog, k2 (41 sts).
Row 30 P.
Row 31 K2, skpo, k12, skpo, k5, k2tog, k12, k2tog, k2 (37 sts).
Row 32 P.
Row 33 K2, skpo, k10, skpo, k5, k2tog, k10, k2tog, k2 (33 sts).
Row 34 P.
Row 35 K2, skpo, k8, skpo, k5, k2tog, k8, k2tog, k2 (29 sts).
Row 36 P.
Row 37 K2, skpo, k6, skpo, k5, k2tog, k6, k2tog, k2 (25 sts).
Row 38 P.
Row 39 K2, skpo, k4, skpo, k5, k2tog, k4, k2tog, k2 (21 sts).
Row 40 P.
Row 41 [K2tog] rep to last st, k1 (11 sts).
Row 42 P.
Thread yarn through stitches.
Neck
Row 43 Using the shaping of horse's head pick up and knit 32 sts from the right side (under the horse's chin) to the left side. You are picking up across the back of the head – 16 sts from left shaping to the centre and 16 sts from centre to right shaping.
Row 44 P.
Row 45 Kfb, k29, kfb, k1 (34 sts).

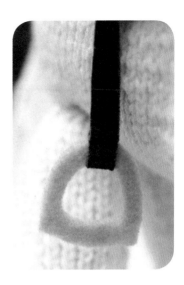

Row 46 P.
Row 47 Kfb, k31, kfb, k1 (36 sts).
Row 48 P.
Rows 49–56 Stocking/stockinette stitch.
Back
Row 57 K24, turn.
Row 58 P12, turn.
Row 59 K12.
Row 60 P12.
Continue on these 12 sts for 28 rows (hold stitches).
Sides
Cut off yarn and rejoin at the inner end of the first 12 sts.
Row 89 (12 sts on needle) pick up and knit 23 sts from right side of

horse's back, k 12 sts on needle, pick up 23 sts from left side of back, k 12 sts on needle (82 sts).
Row 90 P.
Row 91 K.
Row 92 P.
Row 93 Kfb, k79, kfb, k1 (84 sts).
Row 94 P.
Row 95 K.
Row 96 P.
Row 97 Kfb, k81, kfb, k1 (86 sts).
Row 98 P.
Row 99 K.
Row 100 P.
Row 101 Kfb, k83, kfb, k1 (88 sts).
Row 102 P.
Row 103 K.

Row 104 P.
Underside
Row 105 Skpo, skpo, k36, skpo, skpo, k2tog, k2tog, k36, k2tog, k2tog (80 sts).
Row 106 P.
Row 107 Skpo, skpo, k32, skpo, skpo, k2tog, k2tog, k32, k2tog, k2tog (72 sts).
Row 108 P.
Row 109 Skpo, skpo, k28, skpo, skpo, k2tog, k2tog, k28, k2tog, k2tog (64 sts).
Row 110 P.
Row 111 Skpo, skpo, k24, skpo, skpo, k2tog, k2tog, k24, k2tog, k2tog (56 sts).

Row 112 P.
Row 113 Skpo, skpo, k20, skpo, skpo, k2tog, k2tog, k20, k2tog, k2tog (48 sts).
Row 114 P.
Cast off.

Legs (make 4)
Cast on 20 sts.
Rows 1–28 Stocking/stockinette stitch.
Row 29 [K2tog] rep to end of row (10 sts).
Row 30 P.
Thread yarn through stitches.

Ears (make 2)
Cast on 12 sts.
Row 1 K.
Row 2 P.
Row 3 K4, skpo, k2tog, k4 (10 sts)
Row 4 P.
Row 5 K3, skpo, k2tog, k3 (8 sts).
Row 6 P.
Row 7 K2, skpo, k2tog, k2 (6 sts).
Row 8 P.
Row 9 K1, skpo, k2tog, k1 (4 sts).
Thread yarn through stitches.

Making up
Head, neck and body
Sew up body from nose, under the neck and under the body, leaving a gap for stuffing. Fill with stuffing. Sew ears onto each side of head Sew up legs and fill with stuffing. Sew on to the horse.

Finishing off
Tail
Cut 12 strands of yarn measuring 30cm (11¾in). Fold each strand in half.

Sew the yarn to the horse's back around the fold and wrap the yarn around the end of the tail for about 1cm (½in) where it joins the horse so that the tail sticks up.

Fray the yarn using a needle to give a frizzy appearance. Add more threads to the end of the tail if desired.

Mane
Cut a strip of card 3cm (1¼in) wide and 12cm (4¾in) long. Wrap the yarn around the length of the card. The more yarn you use the thicker the mane.

Carefully sew over and under one side of the mane then back again so that every strand is captured in the stitches.

Cut the mane on the other side of the card strip so that there is an even amount of mane each side of the stitches.

Position the mane at the top of horse's head and down the back of the neck with the stitches in the centre. Sew the mane in place using back stitch. Every strand of hair needs to be sewn down. Fray out the yarn using a needle to give a frizzy appearance.

Eyes
Embroider eyes using brown or black yarn.

Horse accessories
Saddle
Cut base of the saddle and stirrup strap in leather and the saddle top in felt using the templates on the following pages.

Cut 2 stirrups and 4 horse shoes from felt. Sew a stirrup to each end of stirrup strap.

Place the base of the saddle onto the middle of the horse's back followed by the stirrups and then the felt saddle.

Sew around the edge of the felt saddle onto the horse so that all 3 sections are secure.

Sew a shoe to each hoof.

Reins
Cut 4 strips of leather.

Wrap a strip around the nose and sew or glue the ends together

Wrap a second strip in front of the ears then down under the chin. Sew or glue the ends together.

Attach a third strip to the side of the nose strip and around the back of the head, below the ears and around to the other side of the nose. Sew or glue the ends to the nose loop.

Attach a 4th strip to each side of the nose strap. This piece is for the reins that the rider would hold on to and should be loose.

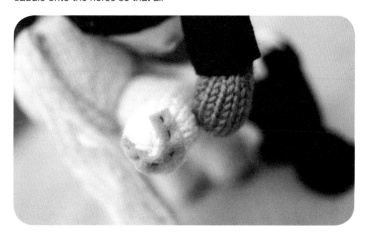

Edward the Equestrian Templates

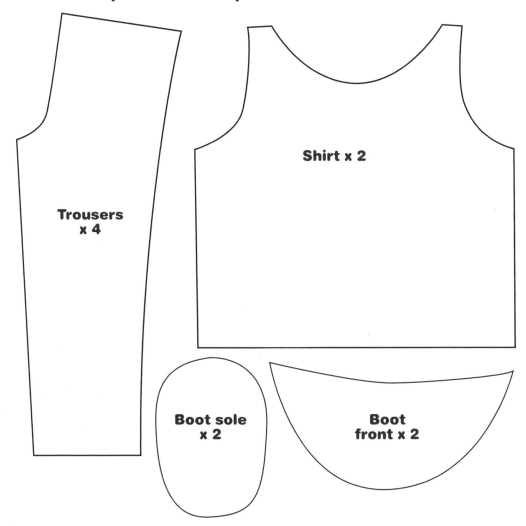

Trousers
x 4

Shirt x 2

Boot sole
x 2

Boot
front x 2

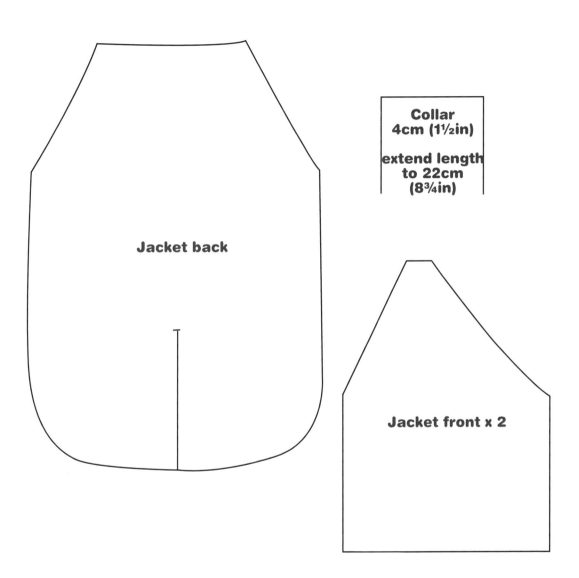

Jacket back

Collar
4cm (1½in)

extend length
to 22cm
(8¾in)

Jacket front x 2

Edward the Equestrian and Harry the Horse Templates

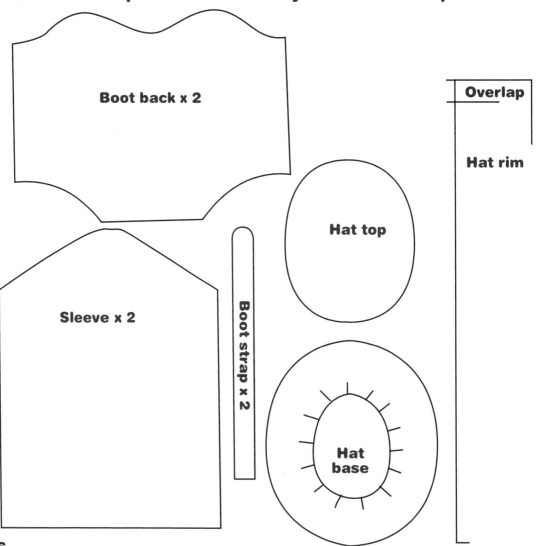

Boot back x 2

Overlap

Hat rim

Hat top

Sleeve x 2

Boot strap x 2

Hat base

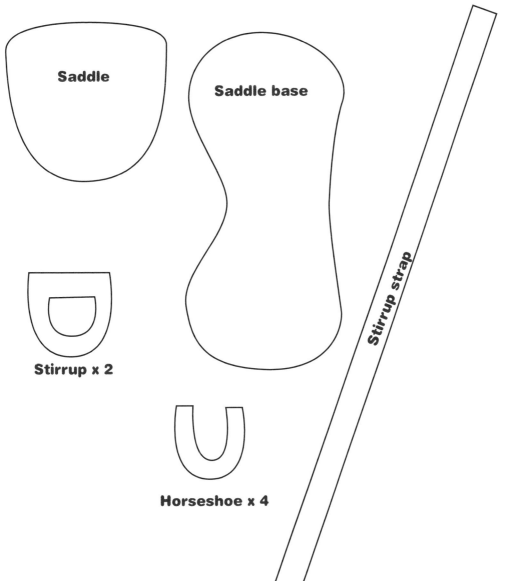

Saddle

Saddle base

Stirrup x 2

Horseshoe x 4

Stirrup strap

Kato the Karateka

Needles

4mm (US size 6) knitting needles

Yarn

50g (2oz) oatmeal DK (this will make 2 dolls)
Oddments of brown yarn for hair, brown or black for eyes and pink for mouth

Other materials

Stuffing
White cotton fabric for trousers and jacket (an old shirt works well for this)
White threat for trousers and jacket
Black felt for the belt

Gauge

22sts and 30 rows to 10cm (4in)

NOTE ON GAUGE

All knitters have slightly different gauge, so it's important to check your gauge so that the outfit your athlete will wear fits properly. If you have more than the stated sts/rows to your 10cm (4in) swatch, then use slightly larger needles. If fewer, use slightly smaller needles.

Finished size

Approximately 33cm (13in) tall.

Abbreviations

K2tog knit the next 2 stitches together
Kfb knit forward and back into the same stitch to make 2 stitches
P2tog purl the next 2 stitches together
Rep repeat
Skpo slip 1, knit 1, pass the slipped stitch over the knitted stitch

Pattern

Head, body and legs

Start at top of head.
Cast on 7 sts.
Row 1 [Kfb] 6 times, k1 (13 sts).
Row 2 P.
Row 3 [Kfb, k1, kfb] 4 times, k1 (21 sts).
Row 4 P.
Row 5 [Kfb, k3, kfb] 4 times, k1 (29 sts).
Row 6 P.
Row 7 K6, [kfb] 2 times, k12, [kfb] 2 times, k7 (33 sts).
Row 8 P.
Rows 9–22 Stocking/stockinette stitch.
Row 23 K6, skpo, k2tog, k12, skpo, k2tog, k7 (29 sts).
Row 24 P.
Row 25 [K2tog, k3, skpo] 4 times, k1 (21 sts).
Row 26 P.
Row 27 K.
Row 28 P.
Body
Row 29 [Kfb, k1] rep to last st, [kfb] (32 sts).
Row 30 P.
Rows 31–54 Stocking/stockinette

stitch.

Row 55 [K2tog, k1] rep to last 2 sts, k2tog (21 sts).

Row 56 P.

Legs

Row 57 K9, k2tog, turn (hold left leg sts and continue on 10 sts for right leg).

Row 58 P.

Rows 59–88 Stocking/stockinette stitch.

Feet

Row 89 K4, [kfb] 2 times, k4 (12 sts).

Row 90 P.

Row 91 K5, [kfb] 2 times, k5 (14 sts).

Row 92 P.

Row 93 K6, [kfb] 2 times, k6 (16 sts).

Row 94 P2tog, p12, p2tog (14 sts).

Row 95 K2tog, k10, k2tog (12 sts).

Row 96 [P2tog] rep to end of row (6 sts).

Thread yarn through remaining sts. Rep on remaining 10 sts for left leg.

Arms (make 2)

Cast on 10 sts.

Rows 1–30 Stocking/stockinette stitch.

Hands

Row 31 K1, [kfb] 2 times, k3, [kfb] 2 times, k2 (14 sts).

Row 32 P.

Rows 33–36 Stocking/stockinette stitch.

Row 37 [K2tog] rep to end of row (7 sts).

Thread yarn through remaining sts.

Making up
Head, body and legs
The head, body and legs are knitted all in one.

Sew down the back of the body and head and fill with stuffing.

Sew down the inner legs to the tips of the toes. Fill with stuffing as you go as the legs are thin.

Arms
Sew up the arm seams, filling with stuffing as you go.

Sew the arms on to the body using the neck shaping to help with positioning.

Hair
Thread a long length of yarn into a thick needle (I used 2 lengths of yarn to make it quicker).

Sew 1cm (½in) stitches around the edge of the head to form the shape of the hairline. Try to work the stitches in the direction that real hair takes.

Fill in the gaps with more stitches until the whole head of hair is covered.

Facial features

Embroider eyes using brown or black yarn.

Using the skin-coloured yarn, pull up 2 stitches just below the centre of the eyes and pull tightly to create the nose. Sew neatly inside the body so that no thread is visible.

Using pink yarn, make 2 stitches just below the nose to create the mouth. You can give the doll different facial expressions by where you choose to place the mouth.

Karate outfit
Trousers
Cut 4 trouser shapes using the template on the following pages. Place the front left leg piece on top of the corresponding back leg piece and repeat with the right leg pieces.

Sew both outside seams using a neat running stitch to join the front leg pieces to the corresponding back leg pieces.

Sew both inside seams using a neat running stitch.

Starting at the top, join 2 front and 2 back pieces together by sewing down the front seam, between the legs and up the back to the waist, ensuring the seams on the inside of the trousers.

around the arm hole ensuring the seam it on the inside. Repeat for the second arm.

Sew up the shoulders.

Turn the jacket right side out so the seams are on the inside.

Fold the trimming and sandwich it all the way down the front and back of the jacket. Sew in place. Using very small and neat running stitches, sew all the way along the trimming in 3 parallel rows (this is not essential but it creates detailing that mimics real karate clothing). Sew all the way around the base of the jacket using a neat running stitch to give a neat finish.

Belt

Cut out a strip of black felt and tie it around the waist of the doll in a knot.

Sew neatly around the waist of the trousers and the bottom of each leg, ensuring the folded down edge is on the inside.

Jacket

Cut out 2 jacket fronts, 1 jacket back, 1 trimming and 2 sleeves in white cotton fabric using the templates on the following pages. Sew both jacket fronts to the back of the jacket. Sew up the shoulders. Sew the bottom of each sleeve using a neat running stich to give a neat edge.

Fold both sleeves in half with the right sides together and stitch to the under arm of the jacket.

Turn the sleeves right side out so the seams are on the inside.

Slip the sleeves into the arm holes so that the arm seams are in line with the side of the jacket seam. Sew the opening of the sleeve

Kato the Karateka Templates

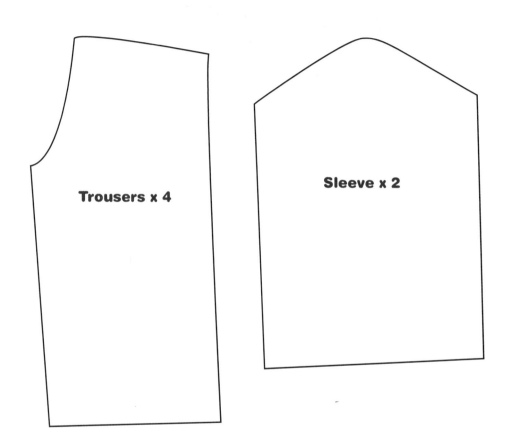

Trousers x 4

Sleeve x 2

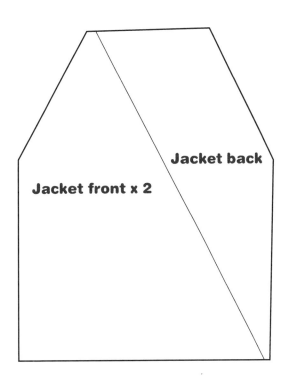

**Trimming
extend
to 34cm
(13½in)**

**6cm
(2½in)**

Jacket front x 2

Jacket back

Rod, Rich, Rick and Ron the Rowers

Needles

4mm (US size 6) knitting needles

Yarn

100g (4oz) skin-coloured DK (this will make 4 dolls)
Oddments of brown yarn for hair, brown or black for eyes and pink for mouth

Other materials

Stuffing
White t-shirt fabric for vest (an old t-shirt works well for this)
Blue ribbon for vest
Blue t-shirt fabric for shorts

Gauge

22sts and 30 rows to 10cm (4in)

NOTE ON GAUGE

All knitters have slightly different gauge, so it's important to check your gauge so that the outfit your athlete will wear fits properly. If you have more than the stated sts/rows to your 10cm (4in) swatch, then use slightly larger needles. If fewer, use slightly smaller needles.

Finished size

Approximately 33cm (13in) tall.

Abbreviations

K2tog knit the next 2 stitches together
Kfb knit forward and back into the same stitch to make 2 stitches
P2tog purl the next 2 stitches together
Rep repeat
Skpo slip 1, knit 1, pass the slipped stitch over the knitted stitch

Pattern

Head, body and legs

Start at top of head.
Cast on 7 sts.
Row 1 [Kfb] 6 times, k1 (13 sts).
Row 2 P.
Row 3 [Kfb, k1, kfb] 4 times, k1 (21 sts).
Row 4 P.
Row 5 [Kfb, k3, kfb] 4 times, k1 (29 sts).
Row 6 P.
Row 7 K6, [kfb] 2 times, k12, [kfb] 2 times, k7 (33 sts).
Row 8 P.
Rows 9–22 Stocking/stockinette

stitch.

Row 23 K6, skpo, k2tog, k12, skpo, k2tog, k7 (29 sts).

Row 24 P.

Row 25 [K2tog, k3, skpo] 4 times, k1 (21 sts).

Row 26 P.

Row 27 K.

Row 28 P.

Body

Row 29 [Kfb, k1] rep to last st, [kfb] (32 sts).

Row 30 P.

Rows 31–54 Stocking/stockinette stitch.

Row 55 [K2tog, k1] rep to last 2 sts, k2tog (21 sts).

Row 56 P.

Legs

Row 57 K9, k2tog, turn (hold left leg sts and continue on 10 sts for right leg).

Row 58 P.

Rows 59–88 Stocking/stockinette stitch.

Feet

Row 89 K4, [kfb] 2 times, k4 (12 sts).

Row 90 P.

Row 91 K5, [kfb] 2 times, k5 (14 sts).

Row 92 P.

Row 93 K6, [kfb] 2 times, k6 (16 sts).

Row 94 P2tog, p12, p2tog (14 sts).

Row 95 K2tog, k10, k2tog (12 sts).

Row 96 [P2tog] rep to end of row (6 sts).

Thread yarn through remaining sts. Rep on remaining 10 sts for left leg.

Arms (make 2)

Cast on 10 sts.

Rows 1–30 Stocking/stockinette stitch.

Hands

Row 31 K1, [kfb] 2 times, k3, [kfb] 2 times, k2 (14 sts).

Row 32 P.

Rows 33–36 Stocking/stockinette stitch.

Row 37 [K2tog] rep to end of row (7 sts).

Thread yarn through remaining sts.

Making up
Head, body and legs
The head, body and legs are knitted all in one.

Sew down the back of the body and head and fill with stuffing. Sew down the inner legs to the tips of the toes. Fill with stuffing as you go as the legs are thin.

Arms
Sew up the arm seams, filling with stuffing as you go.

Sew the arms on to the body using the neck shaping to help with positioning

Hair
Thread a long length of yarn into a thick needle (I used 2 lengths of yarn to make it quicker).

Sew 1cm (½in) stitches around the edge of the head to form the shape of the hairline. Try to work the stitches in the direction that real hair takes.

Fill in the gaps with more stitches until the whole head of hair is covered.

Facial features
Embroider eyes using brown or black yarn.

Using the skin-coloured yarn, pull up 2 stitches just below the centre of the eyes and pull tightly to create the nose. Sew neatly inside the body so that no thread is visible.

Using pink yarn, make 2 stitches just below the nose to create the mouth. You can give the doll different facial expressions by where you choose to place the mouth.

Rower's outfit
Vest
Cut 2 vest shapes in white t-shirt fabric using the template on the

following pages.

Sew both side seams using a neat running stitch.

Sew the front right shoulder strap to the back shoulder strap directly behind it. Repeat on the left side. Turn the vest inside out so that no seams show on outside.

Sew all edges under by 0.5cm (¼in) using a neat running stitch, attaching a ribbon around the neck and arms at the same time. This adds a little detail to an otherwise plain vest.

Shorts

Cut 4 shorts shapes in blue t-shirt fabric using the template on the following page.

Place the front left leg piece on top of the corresponding back leg

piece and repeat with the right leg pieces.

Sew both outside seams using a neat running stitch to join the front leg pieces to the corresponding back leg pieces.

Sew both inside seams using a neat running stitch.

Starting at the top, join 2 front and 2 back pieces together by sewing down the front seam, between the legs and up the back to the waist, ensuring the seams on the inside of the shorts.

Sew neatly around bottom of each leg making sure the folded down edge is on the inside.

Rod, Rich, Rick and Ron the Rowers Templates

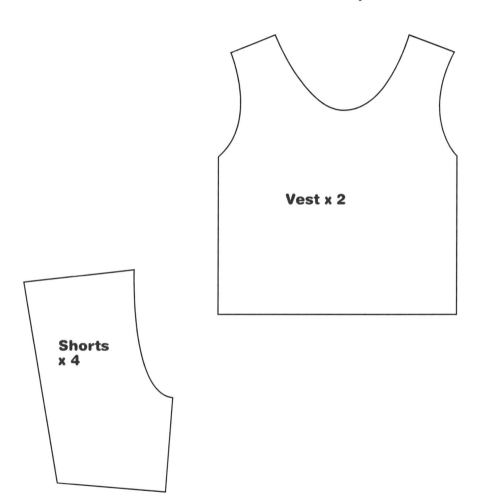

Vest x 2

Shorts
x 4

Su, Sal, Sim, Sam and Sven the Swimmers

Needles
4mm (US size 6) knitting needles

Yarn
100g (4oz) skin-coloured DK (this will make 4 dolls)
Oddments of brown for hair, brown or black and blue for eyes and pink or red for mouth

Other materials
Stuffing

Blue lycra fabric for swimming costume, swimming hat and trunks (an old swimming costume works well for this)
White ribbon for trunks
Blue felt for goggles
Coloured thread for nose clip
Floral lycra fabric for synchronized swimmer's costume
Beads, sequins and sequin strip for synchronized swimmer's costume

Gauge
22sts and 30 rows to 10cm (4in)

NOTE ON GAUGE
All knitters have slightly different gauge, so it's important to check your gauge so that the outfit your athlete will wear fits properly. If you have more than the stated sts/rows to your 10cm (4in) swatch, then use slightly larger needles. If fewer, use slightly smaller needles.

Finished size
Approximately 33cm (13in) tall.

Abbreviations
K2tog knit the next 2 stitches together
Kfb knit forward and back into the same stitch to make 2 stitches
P2tog purl the next 2 stitches together
Rep repeat
Skpo slip 1, knit 1, pass the slipped stitch over the knitted stitch

Pattern
Head, body and legs
Start at top of head.
Cast on 7 sts.
Row 1 [Kfb] 6 times, k1 (13 sts).
Row 2 P.

Row 3 [Kfb, k1,] 4 times, k1
(21 sts).
Row 4 P.
Row 5 [Kfb, k3, kfb] 4 times, k1
(29 sts).
Row 6 P.
Row 7 K6, [kfb] 2 times, k12, [kfb]
2 times, k7 (33 sts).
Row 8 P.
Rows 9–22 Stocking/stockinette
stitch.
Row 23 K6, skpo, k2tog, k12,
skpo, k2tog, k7 (29 sts).
Row 24 P.
Row 25 [K2tog, k3, skpo] 4 times,
k1 (21 sts).
Row 26 P.
Row 27 K.
Row 28 P.
Body
Row 29 [Kfb, k1] rep to last st,
[kfb] (32 sts).
Row 30 P.
Rows 31–54 Stocking/stockinette
stitch.
Row 55 [K2tog, k1] rep to last
2 sts, k2tog (21 sts).
Row 56 P.
Legs
Row 57 K9, k2tog, turn (hold left
leg sts and continue on 10 sts for
right leg).
Row 58 P.
Rows 59–88 Stocking/stockinette
stitch.

Feet
Row 89 K4, [kfb] 2 times, k4
(12 sts).
Row 90 P.
Row 91 K5, [kfb] 2 times, k5
(14 sts).
Row 92 P.
Row 93 K6, [kfb] 2 times, k6
(16 sts).
Row 94 P2tog, p12, p2tog (14 sts).
Row 95 K2tog, k10, k2tog (12 sts).
Row 96 [P2tog] rep to end of row
(6 sts).

Thread yarn through remaining sts.
Rep on remaining 10 sts for left
leg.
Arms (make 2)
Cast on 10 sts.
Rows 1–30 Stocking/stockinette
stitch.
Hands
Row 31 K1, [kfb] 2 times, k3, [kfb]
2 times, k2 (14 sts).
Row 32 P.
Rows 33–36 Stocking/stockinette
stitch.

Hair

Long hair

Wrap the yarn around a large book (the book I used was about 27cm/10¾in tall). The bigger the book, the longer the hair.

Continue wrapping the yarn round the book until it is approximately 4cm (1½in) wide and 0.5–1cm (¼–½in) thick. The more yarn you wrap, the thicker the hair.

Carefully stitch over and under one side of the hair then back again so that every strand of hair is captured in the stitches.

Cut the hair on the other side of the book so that there is an even amount of hair each side of the stitches.

Position the hair at the top of the head with the stitches in the centre. Spread the hair so that it runs down the side and back of the doll's head.

Sew the hair tightly along the top of her head and round the bottom, back and sides of the head. Every strand of hair needs to be sewn down.

Short hair

Thread a large length of yarn onto a thick needle (I used 2 lengths of yarn to make it quicker).

Sew 1cm (½in) stitches around the edge of the head to form the shape

Row 37 [K2tog] rep to end of row (7 sts).
Thread yarn through remaining sts.

Making up
Head, body and legs
The head, body and legs are knitted all in one.

Sew down the back of the body and head and fill with stuffing.

Sew down the inner legs to the tips of the toes. Fill with stuffing as you go as the legs are thin.

Arms
Sew up the arm seams, filling with stuffing as you go.

Sew the arms on to the body using the neck shaping to help with positioning.

of the hairline. Try to work the stitches in the direction that real hair takes.

Fill in the gaps with more stitches until the whole head of hair is covered.

Swimmer's facial features

Embroider eyes using brown or black yarn (I embroidered the eyes once the goggles were in place so that I could make sure the eyes were positioned in the correct place and the doll's would be able to see).

Using the skin-coloured yarn, pull up 2 stitches just below the centre of the eyes and pull tightly to create the nose. Sew neatly inside the body so that no thread is visible.

Using pink yarn, make 2 stitches just below the nose to create the mouth. You can give the doll different facial expressions by where you choose to place the mouth.

Synchronised swimmer's facial features

Nose

Using slightly lighter thread than the doll's skin colour, pull together a few stitches from left to right and pull tightly to create the nose and give the impression of a nose clip.

Eyes

Sew a few small stitches in brown yarn to create the eyes using the nose as a guide. Just above the brown stitches sew a few little stitches in dark blue yarn. Above the blue, sew a few little stitches of a lighter blue to give the impression of eye shadow (you could use any colour you like for the eye shadow but using different tones of the same colour is the most effective).

Mouth

Using pink or red yarn, make a few little stitches below the nose to create the mouth.

Swimmer's outfit

Girl's swimming costume

To cut the swimming costume, fold the fabric in half and pin the template on the following pages to it with the fold of the fabric at the base of the template.

Cut around the edge of the template remembering not to cut along the base fold line.

Sew both side seams using a neat running stitch.

Sew the costume together at the shoulders.

Turn the costume right side out so the seams are on the inside.

Sew around the edges of the legs, neck and arms using a neat running stitch to give a neat finish.

Girl's swimming hat

Cut out the swimming hat in lycra fabric using the template on the following page. (I experimented using a real swimming hat and cutting it up but it was really hard and didn't bend in the way I wanted it to. I gave up but it would look amazing!)

Sew neatly down the back of the hat and turn it right side out so that the stitches are on the inside. You will need to make sure the stitches

are small and neat as the stretchy fabric will pull them apart.

As the dolls' heads are fairly flat you will need to stuff the hat slightly before putting in on her head.

Pin the hat to the front of the head and then around the back.

Sew little stitches under the edge of where the swimming hat will sit using brown yarn. Neatly sew the swimming hat to the head using little stitches.

Boy's trunks

To cut the trunks, fold the fabric in half and pin the template on the following page to it with the fold of the fabric at the base of the template.

Cut around the edge of the template remembering not to cut along the base fold line.

Sew both side seams using a neat running stitch.

Turn the trunks right side out so the seams are on the inside.

Sew around the edges of the legs and waist using a neat running stitch to give a neat finish.

To add extra detail, sew 3 little ribbons down each side of the trunks.

Goggles

Cut out the goggles in blue felt folded in half using the template on the following page and wrap them around the front of the head. Sew in place at each side (you will need to trim the fabric to fit).

Synchronised swimmer's outfit
Swimming costume

To cut the swimming costume, fold the fabric in half and pin the template on the following page to it with the fold of the fabric at the base of the template.

Cut around the edge of the template remembering not to cut along the base fold line.

Sew both side seams using a neat running stitch.

Sew the costume together at the shoulders.

Turn the costume right side out so the seams are on the inside.

Sew around the edges of the legs, neck and arms using a neat running stitch to give a neat finish.

For extra detail, embellish the costume with little beads and sequins using the pattern on the fabric to dictate where these are placed.

Hair decoration

To make the sequined clip and bun, fold the hair up onto the back of the head and slightly twist it. Sew it into place using the same yarn used to create the hair. Cut a 10cm (4in) length of the sequin strip and sew it over the hair stitches to give the impression of a clip.

Su, Sal, Sim, Sam and Sven the Swimmers Templates

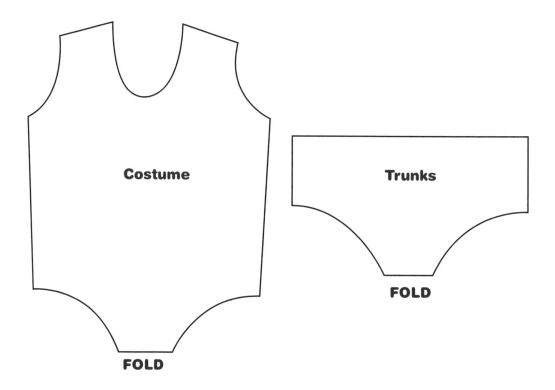

Costume

Trunks

FOLD

FOLD

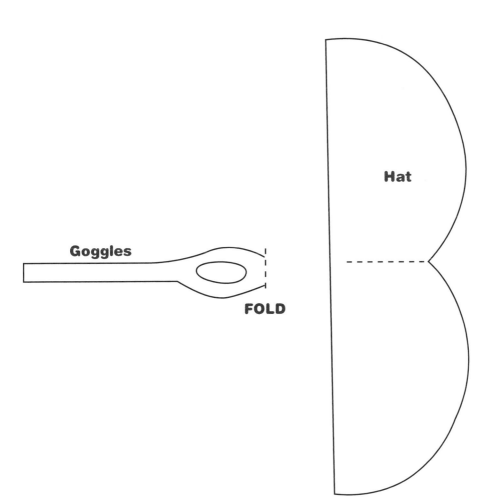

Goggles

FOLD

Hat

Acknowledgments

Thanks to Michelle Bilson, Dan Hughes, Sandra Waehler, Janet Hughes, Martin Duffy, Jenny Tidman, Amy Lane, Sue Collett, Victoria Peat, Hannah Beckley, Jo Wasmuth, Catheryn Hall, Diane Clarke, Karen Baker, Colette Mathers, my lovely MUM, Molly Hopkins, Katie Barton and Zoe Miller.

About the Author

Laura Long graduated in 2003 with a First Class knitted textiles degree from Central St. Martins College of Art and Design. Since then she has been working out of her central London studio designing, making and selling her knitted creations to boutiques and galleries worldwide.

Laura designs, makes and creates patterns and pieces for designers, knitting magazines and pattern books, and her clients have included John Rocha, Rowan yarns, Simply Knitting and Knit Today magazines, and publications such as Collective Knitting and Holiday Knits.

As well as running her own business Laura also takes great pleasure in teaching knitting techniques to others and has taught both machine and hand knitting to people of all ages at Greenwich Community College, Loop in Islington, London, and the Cockpit Arts.

Dolls, fairytales and fantasy played an important part in Laura's childhood, a childhood full of happy, everlasting memories. It is for this reason that she has developed a collection of childhood characters, knitted creatures and dolls with a personality all of their own.

Index

belts 19–20
boots 59, 66
Boxers, Bill and Bob the 30–7

competitor numbers 11
Cyclists, Cindy the 38–45

embroidery 10, 18, 27, 34–5, 42–3, 50, 57, 72, 80, 89
equestrian events
    Edward the Equestrian 54–9, 64–6
    Harry the Handsome Horse 60–3, 67

facemasks (fencing) 51, 53
faces 10, 18, 27, 34–5, 42–3, 50, 57, 72, 80, 89
Fencer, Fiona the 46–53

gloves 35, 51
goggles 90–1, 93
Gymnast, Gloria the 22–9

hair 10, 18, 26–7, 42, 50, 57, 72, 80, 88–9
hair decorations 27, 91
hands 71–2
hats 59, 66, 90, 93
helmets 43, 45
Horse, Harry the Handsome 60–3, 67

jackets 58–9, 65–6, 73–5

Kato the Karateka 68–75
leggings 50–2
leotards 27, 29

moustaches 57–8

reins 63, 67
Rowers, Rod, Rich, Rick and Ron the 76–83
Runner, Reg the 6–13

saddles 63, 67
shirts 58, 64
shoes 11, 13, 18–19, 21, 35, 37, 43–4, 51, 53
shorts 11, 13, 35–7, 43, 45, 81, 83
swim wear 90–2
Swimmers, Su, Sal, Sindy, Sam and Sven the 84–93

trousers 18, 21, 64, 72–4

vests 10–11, 12, 18, 20, 35, 36, 43–4, 51–2, 80–1, 83

Weightlifter, Wayne the 14–21

A DAVID & CHARLES BOOK
© F&W Media International, Ltd 2012

David & Charles is an imprint of F&W
Media International, Ltd
Brunel House, Forde Close, Newton
Abbot, TQ12 4PU, UK

F&W Media International, Ltd is a subsidiary of F+W
Media, Inc.,
10151 Carver Road, Cincinnati OH45242, USA

Text and designs copyright © Laura Long 2012
Layout and Photography © F&W
Media International, Ltd 2012

First published in the UK and USA in 2012
Digital edition published in 2012

Layout of digital editions may vary depending
on reader hardware and display settings.

Laura Long has asserted the right to be identified
as author of this work in accordance with the
Copyright, Designs and Patents Act, 1988.

The author and publisher have made every effort
to ensure that all the instructions in the book are
accurate and safe, and therefore cannot accept
liability for any resulting injury, damage or loss to
persons or property, however it may arise.

Names of manufacturers and product ranges are
provided for the information of readers, with no
intention to infringe copyright or trademarks.

A catalogue record for this book is
available from the British Library.

ISBN-13: 978-1-4463-0232-3 paperback
ISBN-10: 1-4463-0232-6 paperback

ISBN-13: 978-1-4463-5645-6 e-pub
ISBN-10: 1-4463-5645-0 e-pub

ISBN-13: 978-1-4463-5644-9 PDF
ISBN-10: 978-1-4463-5644-2 PDF

Paperback edition printed in Italy by Canale SpA for:
F&W Media International, Ltd
Brunel House, Forde Close, Newton
Abbot, TQ12 4PU, UK

10 9 8 7 6 5 4 3 2 1

Acquisitions Editor: Katy Denny
Editor: James Brooks
Project Editor: Jo Richardson
Senior Designer: Mia Farrant
Photographer: Lorna Yabsley
Production Manager: Bev Richardson

F+W Media publishes high quality books
on a wide range of subjects.
For more great book ideas visit: www.rucraft.co.uk

This book is not published in association with the
Olympic Committee, London Organising Committee for
Olympic Games (LOCOG) or endorsed by LOCOG.